W9-CDG-444

Yellow Umbrella Books are published by Capstone Press
151 Good Counsel Drive, P.O. Box 669, Mankato, Minnesota 56002
http://www.capstone-press.com

Library of Congress Cataloging-in-Publication Data
Trumbauer, Lisa, 1963–
    Who is a friend?/by Lisa Trumbauer; consulting editor, Gail Saunders-Smith.
    p. cm.
    Includes index.
    ISBN 0-7368-0738-1
    1. Friendship in children—Juvenile literature. [1. Friendship.] I. Saunders-Smith, Gail.
II. Title.
BF723.F68 T78   2001
177'.62—dc21   00-036491

Summary: Defines what friends are and describes activities people do with their friends.

Editorial Credits:
Susan Evento, Managing Editor/Product Development; Elizabeth Jaffe, Senior Editor;
    Charles Hunt, Designer; Kimberly Danger and Heidi Schoof, Photo Researchers

Photo Credits:
Cover: International Stock/Dusty Willison; Title Page: Index Stock Imagery and/Richard
Wood; Page 2: International Stock/Dusty Willison; Page 3: Photo Network/Myrleen Ferguson
Cate; Page 4: Photo Network/Myrleen Ferguson Cate (top), Photo Network/CJM Ferguson
(bottom); Page 5: International Stock/Bill Tucker; Page 6: International Stock/Dusty Willison;
Page 7: Index Stock Imagery/John T. Wong (left), Unicorn Stock Photos/Marie Mills (right);
Page 8: Photo Network/Myrleen Ferguson Cate (top left), Pictor (bottom right); Page 9:
International Stock/Joe Willis (left), Photo Network/David N. Davis (right); Page 10: Diane
Meyer (top), Unicorn Stock Photos/Tom McCarthy (bottom); Page 11: International Stock/Bill
Tucker; Page 12: Pictor; Page 13: International Stock/Scott Campbell (left & right); Page 14:
Visuals Unlimited/Jeff Greenberg; Page 15: International Stock/Nicole Katano; Page 16:
International Stock/Joe Willis

1 2 3 4 5 6 06 05 04 03 02 01

Who Is a Friend?

By Lisa Trumbauer

Consulting Editor: Gail Saunders-Smith, Ph.D.
Consultants: Claudine Jellison and Patricia Williams,
Reading Recovery Teachers
Content Consultant: Tammy Huber, Youth Education Director,
North Dakota Farmers Union

Yellow Umbrella Books

an imprint of Capstone Press
Mankato, Minnesota

Who is a friend?
A friend is someone you like.
A friend is someone
who likes you too!

You play with friends.

You talk with friends.

You laugh with friends.

Friends are happy
when you do your best.
Friends want you to be
the best you can be.

Friends cheer you up
when you are sad.
They make you smile.

Friends help you
learn new things.
Friends can help you
learn to read.
Friends can help you
learn to skate.

Friends look different.

Some are short.

Some are tall. Some are old.

Some are young.

Friends like to do
different things.
She likes to play ball.
He likes to color.

Friends do not always like
the same things.

Friends just like to be together.

It is fun to do things
with your friends.
You can have fun
at a birthday party.

Some friends are best friends.
They share many things,
even secrets.

Friends can have
different friends.

Friends do not always
get along.

But friends make up.
This is what friends do.

A friend is someone you like.
A friend is someone
who likes you too!

Tell your friends
that you like them.

Words to Know/Index

Word Count: 193
Early-Intervention Levels: 9–12